ALL ABOUT FOOD

CEREALS, NUTS, & SPICES

Cecilia Fitzsimons

Silver Burdett Press
Parsippany, New Jersey

First American publication
1997 by Silver Burdett Press
A Division of Simon & Schuster
299 Jefferson Road,
Parsippany, NJ 07054-0480

A ZOË BOOK

Original text © 1997 Cecilia Fitzsimons
© 1997 Zoë Books Limited

Devised and produced by
Zoë Books Limited
15 Worthy Lane
Winchester
Hampshire SO23 7AB
England

First published in Great Britain in 1997 by
Zoë Books Limited
15 Worthy Lane
Winchester
Hampshire SO23 7AB

Printed in Belgium by Proost N.V.
Editors: Kath Davies, Imogen Dawson
Design & production: Sterling Associates
Illustrations: Cecilia Fitzsimons

ISBN 0-382-39594-8 (LSB) 10 9 8 7 6 5 4 3 2 1
ISBN 0-382-39599-9 (PBK) 10 9 8 7 6 5 4 3 2 1

Cataloging-in-Publication Data

Fitzsimons, Cecilia
Cereals, nuts, and spices/by Cecilia Fitzsimons.
     p. cm.—(All about food)
Includes bibliographical references and index.
     Summary: Provides information about various kinds of cereal
grains, nuts, and spices, as well as some advice on growing them
and activities and recipes using them.
     1. Cookery (Cereals)—Juvenile literature. 2. Cookery
(Nuts)—Juvenile Literature. 3. Grain—Juvenile Literature.
4. Nuts—Juvenile Literature. 5. Spices—Juvenile Literature.
[1. Grain. 2. Nuts. 3. Spices.] I. Title. II. Series.
TX808.F52 1997   95-32645
841.6'31—dc 20   CIP
                                        AC

Contents

Introduction	4
Wheat	8
Oats and other grains	10
Corn	12
Rice	14
Nuts	16
Walnuts and pecans	18
Other edible nuts	20
Coconuts and Brazil nuts	22
Salt, pepper, and mustard	24
Sweet spices	26
Savory spices	28
Glossary	30
Further reading	31
Index of cereals, nuts, and spices	32

cereals

Introduction

Cereals are the large seeds or grain of some types of grass, such as wheat or oats. They contain a white, floury **starch** that provides most of the energy that our bodies need. This food is called **carbohydrate**.

Nuts are the seeds of some trees, such as hazel or walnut. Each nut is protected by a hard shell. Nuts contain foods called **oils** and **proteins**.

Spices are the dried seeds, roots, or other parts of different plants, such as cinnamon and ginger. They are used in cooking to flavor food. Some spices are used whole, and others are ground into powder.

nuts

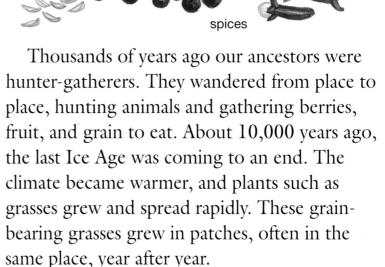

spices

Food facts

Throughout the world cereals are the main, or **staple**, foods. They are the most important part of our diet. These foods are wheat in Europe, corn in the Americas, rice in the Far East, and sorghum and millet in Africa. These staples have not changed in each area since our ancestors first began to grow crops. Today most people eat a mixture of other foods as well as these cereals.

Thousands of years ago our ancestors were hunter-gatherers. They wandered from place to place, hunting animals and gathering berries, fruit, and grain to eat. About 10,000 years ago, the last Ice Age was coming to an end. The climate became warmer, and plants such as grasses grew and spread rapidly. These grain-bearing grasses grew in patches, often in the same place, year after year.

About 6,000 years ago, people found out how to sow the seed from the grain they collected. In this way they could provide food for the next year. They did not need to wander around, looking for food. The first farms and settlements may have been built around these "fields" of wild grain in the Middle East. Farming also developed in North and South America, where the people grew corn, and in the Far East, where the main crop was rice.

The farmers exchanged, or traded, any grain that was left for other goods. Towns and cities grew up around the trading places. This is how **civilizations** developed.

In the kitchen

You will find easy-to-follow recipes in this book. Here are some points to remember when you prepare food:

1. Sharp knives, hot liquids, and pans are dangerous. *Always ask an adult* to help you when you are preparing or cooking food in the kitchen.

2. Before you start, put on an apron and wash your hands.

3. All the ingredients and equipment are listed at the beginning of each recipe. Make sure that you have everything you need before you start.

4. Read the instructions. Measure or weigh the ingredients very carefully.

Think green

We often throw away things that we could use again, or **recycle**. Many cereals, spices, and some nuts are wrapped in packages when they are sold.

If we reused some of our newspapers, cans, bottles, and plastic packaging, we would help to improve our **environment**.

When you read this book, you will find some ideas for things that you can do and make, using cereals, nuts, and spices.

Grow your own cereals, nuts, and spices

Many plants can be grown at home in the garden or in a pot on a balcony or windowsill.

Below are some tips to help you to grow healthy plants. All plants need soil, water, and sunlight for strong, healthy growth.

Sometimes the soil needs to be made richer to feed the plants. Decaying vegetable matter, called compost, is added to it. You can buy **compost** at a garden center, or you can make your own.

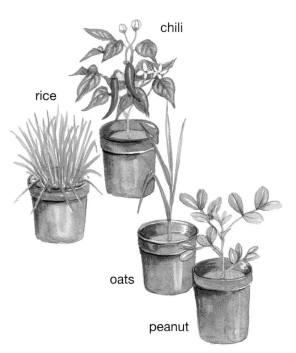

chili

rice

oats

peanut

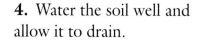

Planting in a pot

1. Take a clean plant pot. Place a few small stones over the holes in the bottom of the pot. This helps water to drain through the pot.

2. Fill the pot with potting soil. Make a hole in the middle it. Gently put in your seed or nut.

3. Push the soil down around the nut or seed. Add more soil and press it down firmly.

4. Water the soil well and allow it to drain.

5. Place the pot in a saucer, dish, or pot holder to catch any water. Stand it on a sunny window ledge or other light place. If planting seeds, place the pot in a plastic bag until the seedlings first appear. Some nuts may take months to **germinate**.

6. Water regularly—once a week is usually enough. Occasionally feed with plant food, bought from a garden center. Follow the instructions on the bottle or packet.

Planting in the garden

You may need to **transplant** your pot-grown plants into the garden.

1. Dig a hole and put some potting soil in the bottom of it.

2. Tap the bottom of your plant pot first to loosen the plant's roots. Remove the plant from its pot.

3. Gently place the plant into the hole. Replace the soil around the roots and press down firmly with your foot. Water and feed the plant regularly.

Seeds

You can buy peanuts, chili and some cereal seeds, such as corn, from grocery stores, garden centers, and mail-order catalogs. Follow the instructions printed on each packet.

Collecting nuts and seeds

You can collect fresh seeds from plants. You can buy rabbit and bird food from a pet shop. Look for undamaged nuts and grain in the pet foods, and collect them.

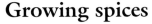

Growing spices

Spices come from **tropical** plants. They are very difficult to grow in cool climates. Always keep these plants indoors. Ginger roots will sprout stiff, grass-like leaves if they are planted in a pot of moist, rich soil. You can try planting whole (unground) spice seeds from health food and grocery stores. These seeds will grow only if they are fresh.

ginger

Wheat

The first farmers sowed wheat and other grains, looked after the crops, and harvested them. They separated the grains from the stalks and the **husks** by **threshing** and **winnowing** it. Then the grain was ground into a powdery flour between two large stones.

Water, milk, or fat was mixed with the flour, and the mixture was cooked on a hot stone near the fire. This is how bread, biscuits and pancakes were made. Today, in spite of our huge fields, farm machinery, grain mills, and bakeries, these foods are still made by the same basic method.

bread wheat

Wheat is a **cross** between two large-seeded grasses called *einkorn* and *spelt*. Today emmer wheat is most like the original wheat plant. It is used for animal food. Different types of wheat have been crossed to produce "bread wheat," used for making bread, biscuits, cakes, and pastries. The world's important wheat-growing areas are in Europe, Central Asia, North America, Australia, and South America.

einkorn   spelt   emmer   bread

There are many different types of bread. They are all made from a basic mixture, or dough, of flour, water, and salt. Bread **dough** needs something to make it rise, such as **yeast** or baking **soda**. These are called leavening agents.

Pasta is a flour dough that is made from durum wheat. It is the staple food in Italy and is made in many different shapes and sizes. The origin of pasta is unclear. It may have come from the Greeks or the Arabs. The traveler Marco Polo may have brought back the recipe after his journeys in China.

spaghetti

pasta

durum wheat

Semolina is also made from durum wheat flour. Couscous is coarse-milled semolina. It is used in Arab cooking.

Food facts

Many special breads are used in religious ceremonies.

A grain of wheat contains 70 percent starch, protein, fat, minerals, **vitamins** A, B, and E, and **fiber**.

White bread was once eaten only by rich people, but is now available to everyone.

In 2,000 BC wheat was one of the five sacred seeds which the emperors of China sowed each spring to honor their gods.

The word "pasta" means "dough."

Salt dough models

You will need:

2 cups of plain flour

1 cup of salt

1 cup of water

a large bowl

a greased cookie sheet

rolling pin, cutters, or modeling tools

paints and varnish

1. Mix the flour and salt in the bowl.

2. Pour in the water. Knead the mixture with your hands for at least 5 minutes.

3. Make a dough model by sticking pieces together with water. You could make a wall hanger by pushing in a hook made from a paper clip.

4. Place your model on a greased cookie sheet. *Ask an adult* to bake it at 200°F (100°C) for an hour for each 1/4 inch (6mm) thickness of dough.

5. After baking, let the model cool. Then paint it. When dry, *ask an adult* to help you varnish it.

Oats and other grains

Most cereals have been grown, or **cultivated**, from about the time that wheat was first grown. Barley may have been the first cereal to be cultivated in the Middle East. Oats and rye probably grew as weeds in the wheat fields. Oats and rye grow in cool climates, while millet and sorghum are tropical crops.

Oat plants are tall, and the grains hang down in feathery clusters. Grown in Europe since the Iron Age, oatmeal is cooked as porridge, oatcakes, and biscuits. Oat husks are used in the manufacture of nylon and other artificial, or **synthetic**, materials.

Rye grows in the coolest climates. It is planted in mountainous areas in Northern Europe and in Russia as far north as the Arctic Circle. Rye is used in Scandinavian crispbread and European black breads.

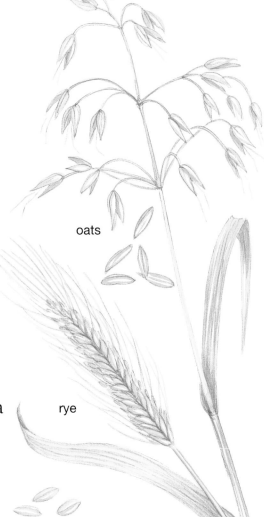

oats

rye

barley

The spike of barley looks like a brush. Each grain bears a long bristle, or filament, called an awn. Barley sprouts are dried to produce malt. They are used to brew beer and to make malted milk and flavorings. Pearl barley is dehusked grain.

Think green

Organic flour is ground from cereals that are grown without chemical fertilizers and pesticides. Look for bread made from organic flour in stores.

Cut down on waste and feed scraps of bread to wild birds.

Buckwheat is the only common cereal that is not made from a member of the grass family. The seeds of this plant are roasted and ground to make buckwheat flour, which is used to make pancakes.

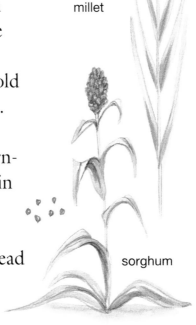
buckwheat

millet

Millet has been grown since ancient times in Southern Europe and in Asia. In Africa it is made into a porridge called mealie. Some millet is sold in pet shops, as bird seed.

Sorghum is a tall, corn-like plant that is grown in Africa, Asia, and other tropical areas. Sorghum flour is used to make bread and porridge.

sorghum

Food facts

Scottish warriors were feared by their enemies because they could march long distances while eating nothing but oatcakes.

For a healthy diet, eat wholegrain bread because it contains the most fiber.

In India, barley is used to celebrate the birth of a child.

Make your own muesli

You will need:

6 oz (175 g) rolled oats

2 oz (50 g) wheatflakes

1½ oz (40 g) bran

2 oz (50 g) raisins or dates

2 oz (50 g) sunflower seeds

5 oz (150 g) chopped mixed nuts

4 oz (100 g) chopped dried apricots

1 oz (25 g) dried banana chips

---

a mixing bowl

a large spoon

an airtight container

1. Place all the ingredients in the bowl and mix well together.

2. Store in an airtight container until needed.

3. Serve with milk or yogurt.

Corn

Corn was first cultivated in Central America about 6,000 years ago. It soon became the staple food in North and South America. Now it is grown all over the world. Corn grows easily in poor soils. It is eaten both as a vegetable (sweet corn) and as a cereal.

Corn is a tall, reedlike plant, which can grow to 6 feet (2m) high. It has wide, grassy leaves and strong stems. The male flowers grow in a feathery tassel at the top of the stem. The female flowers grow at the base of the leaves and later develop into cobs.

There are many different varieties of corn. The seeds may be floury, sweet (as in sweet corn), hard, dented, white, yellow, black, or red. Popcorn has hard seeds that burst when they are heated. Sweet corn is eaten fresh, or it can be frozen or canned.

male flower

corn

female flower

an ear of corn

Dry, ripe corn kernels are rolled or ground into the flour known as corn flour. Corn meal and corn flour are used in Mexican recipes to make tortillas, tacos, corn bread, and corn chips. Corn oil is used as cooking oil.

Grow your own sweet corn

Buy a packet of corn seeds and follow the instructions. Seedlings planted in spring will grow into huge plants by the end of the summer. Soon you will be eating your own tasty corn.

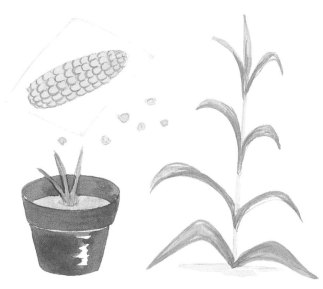

Corn plants "drown" if they are flooded for more than 24 hours. Do not over-water them.

Food facts

Columbus brought corn to Europe from the Americas in 1493. By 1521, Magellan had carried corn to the Philippines, and by 1555 people were growing it in China.

Corn grains contain starch, protein, sugar, and oil.

Cornflakes were the first commercial breakfast cereal produced by W. K. Kellogg.

Italian corn mush is called *polenta*.

Make your own popcorn

You will need:

popping corn

cooking oil

salt, butter, or molasses

---

a saucepan with a tight-fitting lid

a teaspoon

1. Pour a teaspoon of oil into the pan. Add a spoonful of corn and put on the saucepan lid.

2. *Ask an adult* to heat the pan, shaking it over the heat. You will hear the corn popping inside. Do not take off the lid until the corn has finished popping.

3. Tip the corn into a large container. Sprinkle it with salt, melted butter, or molasses.

Rice

Rice has been grown in China and India for nearly 8,000 years. It is the staple crop for most of Asia and is grown in Europe, Australia, and the United States.

Some rice is grown in dry fields, but most is planted in flooded paddies. Steplike terraces of paddies are found in some mountainous areas of Asia. Many people are needed to plant and weed the rice by hand. The fields are drained just before harvest when the rice is cut, threshed, milled, and then polished.

rice plant

In California, rice seed is sown by scattering seed from planes as they fly over the vast fields. At harvest time a huge combine, driven by one person, can harvest 275 tons of rice a day.

There are at least 1,300 **varieties** of rice. Patna, Basmati, and Thai are long-grain varieties. Japanese, Italian, and red rice are short-grained, sticky varieties. Rice is cooked as grains, parboiled, flaked, or ground into rice flour. Brown rice is unpolished and still has its fibrous seed coat.

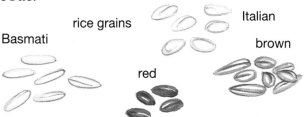

rice grains

Basmati

Italian

brown

red

Food facts

Rice feeds half the world's population.

Rice is high in carbohydrates, but it contains less protein than other cereals.

The Chinese daily greeting "How do you do?" is actually "Have you eaten your rice?"

A *shimenawa* is a thick rope of rice straw. In Japan, people hang them over the door of a house or temple to protect it from evil.

Rice is an important part of Indian, Chinese, Japanese, and Thai cookery. In Europe, rice is traditionally eaten as *risotto* in Italy, *paella* in Spain, and milk puddings in Great Britain. Commercially, rice is toasted and popped to make "rice crispies." They are used in breakfast cereals, sweets, and desserts.

Wild rice is not related to true rice. It is a tall water reed that grows in the swamps and shallow lakes of North America. Wild rice was a staple grain for Native Americans and is still collected in the traditional way. The seeds are shaken from the reeds by hand into the bottom of a small boat. This is why wild rice is a luxury product and is very expensive to buy.

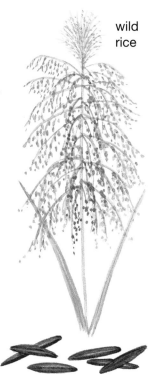

wild rice

Grow your own rice

1. Brown rice will germinate if it is not too old. Sow some seeds onto a pot of damp, peat-free soil. Place the pot in a plastic bag and put it on a window ledge.

2. The seeds should sprout after about two weeks. When the seedlings are 4 in (10 cm) tall, transplant them into a watertight pot.

3. Water well and keep the soil covered with water. Keep the pot in a warm, sunny place.

Make your own rice crispie cakes

You will need:

6 oz (175 g) rice crispies

2 oz (50 g) butter

1 oz (25 g) cocoa powder

2 level tablespoons light corn syrup

---

a saucepan

a teaspoon

a tablespoon

paper baking cups

1. Put the butter, syrup, and cocoa into a saucepan.
2. *Ask an adult* to help you to warm the ingredients over low heat until they melt. Mix well.

3. Remove the pan from the heat. Add the rice crispies and carefully mix together until the crispies are all coated with the sauce.
4. Place two teaspoons of the cake mixture into each baking cup. Leave them to cool.

Nuts

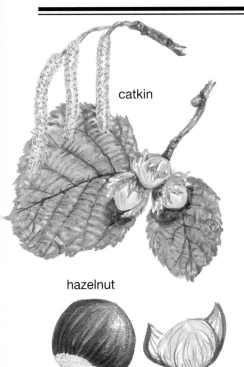

catkin

hazelnut

Nuts are still collected from wild trees, but they are now also grown in orchards. Hundreds of years ago the Arab people used nuts in cooking and in desserts. This tradition spread to Europe during the Middle Ages. At the same time, nuts such as pecans were an important food for Native American peoples.

The hazel is a small tree or bush. There are several types, or **species**, including cobnuts from Northern Europe and filberts from Turkey. Male hazel flowers are the long catkins known as lambs' tails. Hazelnuts are eaten raw or roasted. They are used in cakes, biscuits, and desserts.

The sweet chestnut tree is a large tree that originally grew in southern Europe. It is now planted worldwide for its wood and nuts. Up to three chestnuts grow inside each prickly green case. Chestnuts are usually roasted or cooked as a vegetable in soups and stews. Chestnut stuffing is traditionally served with roast turkey.

catkin

sweet chestnut

nut

fruit

almond

fruit

Almonds are related to peaches and apricots. The nut is actually the seed inside the fruit. Almonds are used raw or roasted, in both sweet and savory dishes. Sugared almonds are one of the oldest sweets and may date from Roman times. Ground almonds are used to make almond paste, or marzipan.

Pine nuts grow inside the cones of the Mediterranean stone pine tree. These nuts are used in Italian cooking, in dishes such as *pesto*, and in soups. In North America, pine nuts are obtained from the pinyon pine.

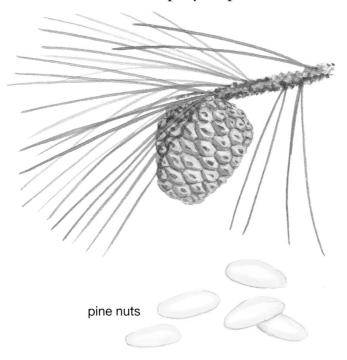

pine nuts

Food facts

Hazelnut shells are used to make plywood and the floor covering called linoleum.

Chestnuts contain more starch and less fat than other nuts. Chestnut flour is still used to make cakes.

Almonds are rich in calcium, which our bodies need for strong teeth and bones.

Almond oil is used in cosmetics.

A famous French way of preserving chestnuts in syrup is called *marrons glacés* (candied chestnuts).

Make your own candies—Hazelnut clusters

You will need:

3 oz (85 g) shelled hazelnuts

8 oz (125 g) semisweet chocolate

a heat proof bowl or
  a double boiler

a saucepan

a teaspoon

paper baking cups

1. Break up the chocolate and put into the top pan of the double boiler.

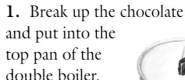

2. Place the pan over the bottom pan of hot (not boiling) water.

3. Stir the chocolate until it is melted.

4. Add the hazelnuts. Stir well. Place teaspoons of the mixture into paper baking cups.

5. Allow to cool and set.

Walnuts and pecans

Walnuts and their relatives are tall trees with leaves that are divided into a number of smaller leaflets. They have short, green catkins and bear tough, green fruit. Inside the fruit is a hard-shelled nut. The surface of the nut is usually wrinkled.

The common or English walnut trees first grew in Iran. Now they are widely planted for their wood and nuts. They are grown as a crop, for sale, in France and California. Whole young fruits, picked while the shell is still soft, are used to make pickled walnuts. Walnuts are eaten whole or used in baking and desserts. Walnut oil is used in salad dressings.

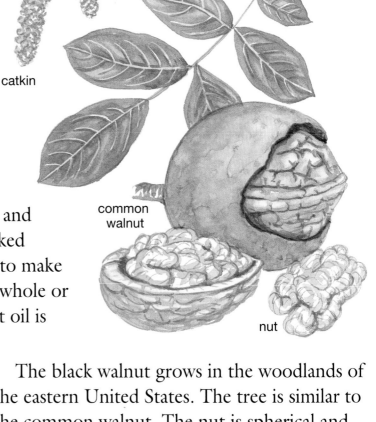

fruit

catkin

common walnut

nut

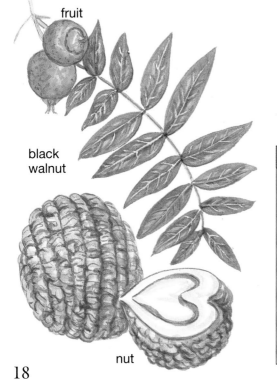

fruit

black walnut

nut

The black walnut grows in the woodlands of the eastern United States. The tree is similar to the common walnut. The nut is spherical and has a very thick and hard shell. It has a strong walnut taste.

Food facts

There are 20 different species of trees in the walnut family.

Walnut wood has beautiful grain patterns and is used to make fine furniture.

Nuts are good for you! Most nuts are rich in proteins, **minerals**, vitamins, and fiber.

Pecans also come from North America. These trees grow clusters of oval fruit. Each nut has a thin, smooth shell. Pecans are eaten salted or fresh and baked in pecan pie. They are also used in breads, cakes, ice cream, candy, and vegetarian cookery.

The butternut tree is also called a white walnut. It comes from the United States, but is less well-known than other nut trees. Its egg-shaped nuts are used in the same way as walnuts and pecans.

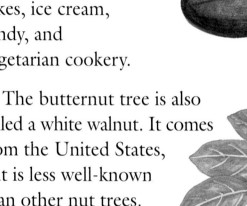

fruit

pecan

nut

fruit

Grow your own nut tree

1. Fill a pot with potting soil. Plant a nut in it.

2. Water the soil, place the pot in a plastic bag, and leave it in a light place.

3. Be patient! Germination can take several months. Some nuts may not germinate at all if they are too old.

4. Repot the seedling into a larger pot. Eventually you will need to plant your tree outside.

Bacon and walnut salad

You will need:

lettuce leaves
  (several varieties if possible)

a bunch of watercress

salad dressing (You will find a recipe for salad dressing on page 25, or use a bottled dressing.)

salt and pepper

4 oz (125 g) bacon, cut into small pieces

4 oz (125 g) walnut pieces

walnut or olive oil

---

a frying pan

a wooden spoon

a serving bowl

1. Wash and drain the lettuce leaves and watercress. Arrange pieces of the salad leaves in the serving bowl. Sprinkle with salad dressing, and season with salt and pepper.

2. *Ask an adult* to help you to fry the bacon pieces. Add the walnut pieces. Stir and cook for 1 minute.

3. Carefully spoon the hot bacon and walnut mixture over the salad. Eat immediately with crusty bread.

Other edible nuts

Some edible nuts are roasted and salted so we can eat them as snacks. They are also used in baking, in confectionery, in vegetarian, and in oriental cookery.

The peanut is not a true nut but is related to peas and beans. Two or three peanuts grow in a pod called the shell. Peanuts grow underground, which is why they are also called groundnuts. Peanuts are eaten raw or roasted. They are ground up to make peanut butter. Groundnut oil is used for cooking, in salads, and to make margarine.

flower

peanut shell

peanuts

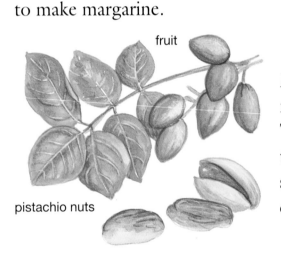

fruit

pistachio nuts

Pistachio nuts come from the Middle East, Mediterranean countries, and California. The male and female flowers grow on separate trees. These nuts are bright green and grow inside a thin, hard shell. Pistachios are eaten roasted and salted. They are also used in baking, confectionery, and to flavor ice cream.

Macadamia nuts come from the rain forests of Queensland, Australia. These nuts are now also grown commercially in Hawaii. Hanging sprays of white flowers develop into clusters of green fruit with round, brown nuts inside them.

fruit

flower

macadamia nuts

Food facts

The oil in cashew-nut shells causes blisters. It is used as waterproofing and as a preservative.

Roasted peanuts are rich in protein, which our bodies need for growth and to stay healthy.

Some people become ill when they eat peanuts. Their bodies are **allergic** to them.

Cashew nuts originally came from South America but are now grown in India, Europe, and Africa. Each nut hangs beneath a fleshy fruit called a cashew apple. Cashew nuts must be roasted before they are eaten, to remove the poisonous oil found in their shells.

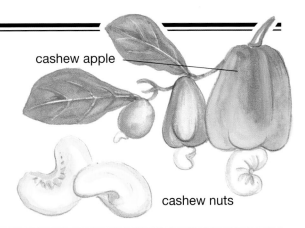
cashew apple

cashew nuts

Make a bird feeder

Warning

Do not feed peanuts to birds during the nesting season. Whole peanuts can choke baby chicks.

You will need:

an empty plastic soft-drink bottle + cap

3 wooden skewers or kebab sticks

string, 12 in (30 cm) long

scissors

8 oz (225 g) shelled peanuts

1. Pull off and throw away the black plastic base of the bottle, if it has one.

2. *Ask an adult* to help you to make a hole in the bottle cap. Fold the string in half and push the loop through the hole from the inside.

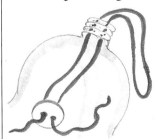

3. Knot the ends of the string around a stick or button, small enough to fit inside the cap. Screw the cap back on.

4. *Ask an adult* to help you cut the bottom of the bottle off with scissors, about 2 in (5 cm) from the base.

5. Turn the bottle upside down and fill it with peanuts to within 2 in (5 cm) from the top.

6. Take the piece of bottle you have cut off and push it into the bottle, upside down, until the two cut surfaces are level.

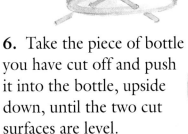

7. *Ask an adult* to help you to push the three wooden sticks right through the bottle and base, so that they radiate like the spokes of a wheel.

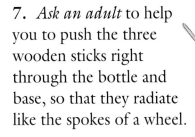

8. Cut six small holes in the bottle, each just bigger than a nut.

9. Hang the bottle up and watch the birds feed.

Coconuts and Brazil nuts

Coconut trees are the coastal palm trees that grow on tropical beaches. Each tree can grow to a height of about 80 feet (25 m). The coconut itself grows inside a huge, fibrous case that is as big as a football. When ripe, the nut falls into the sea and floats away until it is washed up on another beach. There it will germinate and grow. At one end of a coconut, there are round shapes that look like a face with two eyes. These are soft parts of the shell. The roots and shoot will grow through them at germination. Coconuts are harvested by people who climb right to the top of the trees and cut the fruit down with large knives.

Coconut flesh is white and hard. The center of the nut is hollow. It is full of sugary coconut milk.

Coconut flesh is eaten fresh or dried. Shredded, dried coconut is sold as flaked coconut. It is used in baking, confectionery, and to flavor some Indian, Chinese, and Thai dishes.

The coconut seed, or kernel, contains a lot of oil. The oil is taken out of the dried kernel, or copra. It is sold for cooking oil. It is also used to make margarine, soap, and cosmetics.

The oil cake that remains after the oil has been taken out is fed to animals. The fruit husk is used to make coconut matting, doormats, and compost. Nothing is wasted.

coconut tree

fruit

coconut

Brazil nuts

Brazil nuts grow on tall rain forest trees in South America. About 24 hard nuts are packed inside a thick, woody fruit, called an *ourico*. It looks like a cannon ball and does not break when it falls to the ground.

Brazil nuts are rich in oil, which is used for cooking and to make cosmetics. Brazil nuts are eaten raw or used in cakes and candies.

ourico

Brazil nut

Food facts

A single Brazil nut tree can produce 1,100 lb (500 kg) of nuts each harvest.

Brazil nuts contain 70 percent fat and 14 percent protein.

Chilled, fresh milk from a young green coconut is a favorite drink in Brazil.

Think Green

Use coconut fiber compost rather than peat compost to help to save peat bogs and wetlands.

Make coconut candy squares

You will need:

4 tbs (60 ml) milk
4 tbs (60 ml) water
1 lb (450 g) sugar
½ oz (15 g) butter
4 oz (125 g) flaked coconut
½ teaspoon vanilla flavoring
a cup of water

---

a square pan lined with nonstick paper
a saucepan
a wooden spoon
a teaspoon
a knife

1. Pour the water and milk into a saucepan. *Ask an adult* to help you heat the liquid until it boils.

2. Add the sugar and butter. Stir until the sugar and butter have melted.

3. *Ask an adult* to boil the mixture for 10 minutes.

4. Using a teaspoon, drop a little of the mixture into the cup of water. When cooked, it should form a soft ball.

5. *Ask an adult* to remove the saucepan from the heat. Add the coconut and vanilla. Stir well until thick and creamy.

6. *Ask an adult* to pour the mixture into the lined pan, spread it out, and leave it in a cool place to set.

7. Mark out squares in the mixture with the knife before it has set too hard.

8. Cut into squares when cold.

Salt, pepper, and mustard

Salt, pepper, and mustard are used every day, but where do they come from?

Salt is a mineral called sodium chloride. It is the only pure mineral that we eat. Sea salt comes from sea water that is trapped in shallow pools in coastal marshes. As the water dries up, or **evaporates**, in the sun, salt crystals form. Some sea salt is produced by heating sea water in large vats. Rock salt is mined underground. It is found in rock that was once part of a prehistoric sea. Other salt comes from natural salt springs. Until about 150 years ago, the only way to preserve food was to salt or dry it.

Bacon and ham are meats that are preserved in salt. Other foods, such as gherkins, are pickled in salt water, or brine.

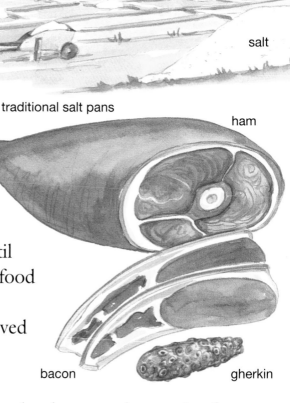

salt

traditional salt pans

ham

bacon

gherkin

green peppercorns

white peppercorns

ground pepper

black peppercorns

Pepper has been used as a spice for more than 2,000 years. Pepper vines come from India and now also grow in Southeast Asia and Brazil. Pepper is ground from green berries called peppercorns. They grow in long, hanging clusters. Black peppercorns are the sun-dried green berries. White peppercorns are red berries that are left to ripen on the vine. After picking, they are soaked, and the red skins are removed. Green peppercorns are soft, unripe berries that are usually pickled in brine.

Mustard has been made for about 2,000 years. The seeds of these cabbage-like plants are ground and mixed with water, wine, or oil to make a paste. The paste is served with meat and other foods. Mustard is also used in cooking to give a "hot" flavor to sauces, pickles, and chutneys.

ground mustard

mustard seeds

Food facts

The early Chinese used coins made from salt for currency.

An English word that means a wage or payment is *salary*. It comes from the Latin word for salt, *sal*. Roman soldiers were paid in salt.

The saying "not worth your salt" originally meant that a tough piece of meat was not worth preserving.

In the Middle Ages, the word "pepper" meant any spice.

A famous mustard is produced near Dijon in France.

Make a vinaigrette salad dressing

You will need:

pinch of salt

1 tsp whole grain (Dijon) mustard

1 tsp ground black pepper

2 tbs wine vinegar

6 tbs olive, walnut, or groundnut oil

a screw-top jar

1. Put the salt, pepper, and mustard into the jar.

2. Add the vinegar. Screw on the lid of the jar and shake.

3. Add the oil to the jar and shake well. Shake until the dressing becomes slightly thickened and cloudy.

4. Pour a little dressing over the salad and mix it in, just before you eat it.

Find your favorite flavor

You can make different flavors of salad dressing by changing the ingredients you use. You could add crushed garlic or herbs when you shake up the dressing.

Different kinds of vinegars and oils will also change the taste of your salad dressing. You could try white or red wine vinegar, cider vinegar, lemon vinegar, raspberry vinegar, or vinegar with herbs such as tarragon. Try hazelnut, raisin, or virgin olive oils.

Keep a note of your favorite ingredients for your salad dressing.

Sweet spices

For thousands of years spice and silk **caravans** traveled overland from China and India to the city of Istanbul. There they traded goods with Mediterranean merchants. Every year ships from northern Europe sailed to the Mediterranean to trade. They returned just before Christmas loaded with spices, dried fruits, almonds, oranges, lemons, brandy, and sherry. These ingredients are still used today in Christmas baking recipes throughout Europe. European settlers took these traditional recipes with them when they emigrated to the Americas, Australia, and other countries around the world.

clove flowers

Cloves are the dried flower buds from a tree of the myrtle family. They first grew in Indonesia. Later they were grown in Zanzibar and Madagascar. Cloves are used powdered or whole in sweet and savory dishes, and in baking and pickling.

cloves

cinnamon

Cinnamon trees are related to laurel. The inner bark is removed by hand, curled into long quills, and then dried. Pieces of cinnamon quill are used to flavor liquids or ground and used in baking. Cinnamon was probably first grown in India, but is now grown in Sri Lanka, China, the Seychelles, and Madagascar.

cinnamon quills

Ginger is the knobbly underground stem, or **rhizome**, of a reedlike plant from the forests of Southeast Asia. It is used fresh or canned to give a "hot" flavor when cooking sweet and savory dishes. The dried, ground spice is a popular flavoring for cakes and cookies. Candied ginger is used in sweets and other confectionery.

ground ginger

fresh ginger

Nutmeg trees grow in the Moluccas, islands of Indonesia. Inside a fleshy husk, the nut is covered with a bright red case. This case is dried to make another different flavored spice, called mace. Nutmeg is used to flavor milk in puddings and sauces.

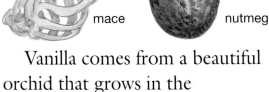

fruit

mace

nutmeg

Vanilla comes from a beautiful orchid that grows in the rain forests of Central America. Vanilla is also grown in Madagascar and the West Indies. The fruit, vanilla pods, produce their characteristic flavor only when they have been cured and dried. Vanilla is used to flavor ice cream, candies, and other desserts.

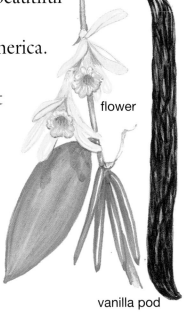

flower

vanilla pod

Food facts

Clove oil is known as a cure for toothache.

Cinnamon was used in cosmetics by the ancient Egyptians. Cinnamon oil is used in perfume today.

More than 500 years ago, the Aztecs in Mexico added vanilla to their hot chocolate drinks.

Make spice cookies

You will need:

8 oz (225 g) flour

4 oz (125 g) butter

4 oz (125 g) sugar

1 tsp mixed spices

½ tsp ground cinnamon

1 beaten egg

a mixing bowl

a wooden spoon

a rolling pin

cookie cutters

a greased cookie sheet

1. *Ask an adult* to preheat the oven to 350°F (180°C).

2. Put the flour, sugar, and spices into a mixing bowl. Cut in the butter until the mixture looks like fine bread crumbs.

3. Add the egg and knead the mixture into dough.

4. Put the dough into a plastic bag and chill in the refrigerator for 30 minutes.

5. Use the rolling pin to roll out the dough thinly on a floured surface.

6. Cut out the dough into cookie shapes. Place them on the cookie sheet.

7. *Ask an adult* to put the cookies in the oven and bake them for 10 to 15 minutes.

Savory spices

Many spices are used to flavor savory foods around the world. Some of these dishes are hot and fiery, while others are mild and fragrant.

Saffron is the most expensive spice of all. It was first used in the Middle East. Saffron is produced from the orange stigmas of a purple crocus flower. There are only three stigmas in each flower, and several thousand flowers must be picked by hand to make 1 pound (450 g) of saffron. Saffron also makes a delicate yellow dye. Saffron is used to flavor and color rice, fish dishes, cakes, and breads.

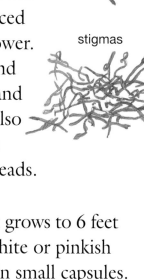

saffron

flower

stigmas

Sesame is a tall plant. It grows to 6 feet (2m) in height and has white or pinkish flowers. The seeds grow in small capsules. They are rich in oil and are used in baking and in Arab and Asian cookery.

Chili is the hottest spice of all. The chilies are the fruit of small red peppers that were first grown in Mexico. Columbus took them to Europe, and they soon spread to the Mediterranean, Africa, India, and the Far East.

sesame

fruit

sesame seeds

chili

chili powder

Chili powder is ground from dried peppers. Paprika is less fiery. It is ground from dried sweet peppers. It is a popular spice in Hungarian cookery.

Turmeric is ground from the rhizomes of an East Indian herb. It is bright yellow and is used to color and flavor food, such as mustard.

turmeric powder

Allspice is the fruit of the West Indian pimento tree. It tastes like a mixture of several other spices, which is why it is called "allspice." It is sometimes called "Jamaica pepper."

flower

allspice

fruit

Curry powder

In India and other Asian countries, many dishes are highly spiced. A curry sauce is flavored with a mixture of spices. The spices include turmeric, coriander seed, ginger, chili, pepper, mustard, cloves, cumin, cardamom, and fenugreek. Some of these spices are ground up to make a special curry powder to flavor food.

curry spices

Food facts

In India, turmeric is mixed with milk to form a cooling lotion for the face and eyes.

Saffron Walden is a town in Essex, England. Its precious saffron fields were protected by high walls. They were literally "walled in."

Anise is used to flavor cough syrups and candies.

Make a sweet-smelling spice picture

You will need:

poster paper

a pencil

glue

Whole dried spices such as peppercorns; cloves; cinnamon sticks; vanilla pod; sesame seeds; allspice; chili peppers; mace; star anise; mustard seeds; coriander seeds; cardamom; fenugreek seeds; nutmeg.

1. Draw a pattern or design on the poster paper.

2. Keeping the paper on a flat surface, stick spices onto your design with glue. Position the spices close together so that all the design is covered.

3. Don't move the paper until the glue is completely dry.

4. Display in a warm place. It will make the room smell spicy.

Glossary

allergic: describes the state in which the body is sensitive to, or reacts badly to, substances that are normally harmless.

caravan: a group of people traveling together for safety, as through a desert. Traders often traveled in caravans, carrying goods.

carbohydrate: a food substance such as starch or sugar that is energy rich.

civilization: a group of people who live by the same laws and customs.

compost: a mixture of decaying vegetable matter for enriching soil.

cross: growing a plant from two different parent plants.

cultivate: to grow on a farm or in a garden.

dough: the mixture of flour, water, salt, and yeast, which is cooked to make bread.

environment: everything around us, such as air, water, and land.

evaporate: when water seems to dry up, it is really changing into small droplets of water, or vapor, in the air.

fertilizer: a substance, often made from chemicals, that is added to the soil in order to produce more crops.

fiber: coarse, bulky food, such as bran and fruit peel. Fiber helps digestion.

germinate: when a seed starts to grow into a plant.

husk: the outer covering of some fruits, grains, and seeds.

mineral: a substance without life, such as metals and crystals that are found in the earth.

oil: a greasy liquid that is pressed from olives or other fruits and nuts, used in cooking.

pesticide: a substance made of chemicals that kills pests such as insects that damage plants.

protein: an important substance in certain foods that people and animals need to live and grow.

recycle:	to make something new from something that has already been used.
rhizome:	an underground stem producing roots and leafy shoots.
soda:	a chemical. Baking soda is made of sodium bicarbonate.
species:	a type of animal or plant.
staple:	the most important type of crop or food in a particular area.
starch:	a white, high-energy food substance, without taste or smell, which is found in foods such as bread and potatoes.
synthetic:	a substance or material that is made by people and is not produced naturally.
thresh:	to beat. Grain is separated from its husks by threshing.
transplant:	to replant in another place.
tropical:	from the lands near the equator, where the heat from the sun is strongest. We draw lines on maps to show the position of the tropics. Plants from the tropics grow best in hot, wet places.
variety:	a type of animal or plant within a species.
vitamins:	small amounts of special substances in foods that people and animals need for good health. Most nuts contain vitamin B.
winnow:	to separate grain from husks, or chaff, by blowing it away. The husks are lighter than the grain.
yeast:	a single-celled organism. It is added to dough to make the mixture rise.

Further reading

Food and Feasts: With the Aztecs by Imogen Dawson. New Discovery Books, 1995. This introduction to the ancient Aztec civilization examines the food the people ate, their customs, feasts and festivals and includes authentic, delicious recipes.

Eat Well by Miriam Moss. Crestwood House 1993. Young readers will learn how to plan a diet to help them stay healthy and will get practical advice that can help improve their confidence and well-being.

Index of cereals, nuts, and spices

allspice 29
almonds 16, 17, 26
anise 29

barley 10, 11
black peppercorns 24
Brazil nuts 22, 23
buckwheat 11
butternuts 19

cardamom 29
cashews 20, 21
chestnuts 16, 17
chili 7, 28, 29
cinnamon 4, 26, 27, 29
cloves 26, 27, 29
cobnuts 16
coconuts 22, 23
coriander 29
corn 4, 5, 7, 12, 13
cumin 29
curry powder 29

durum wheat 9

emmer wheat 8

fenugreek 29
filberts 16

ginger 4, 7, 26, 29
green peppercorns 24
groundnuts 20

hazelnuts 4, 16, 17

Jamaica pepper 29

Macadamia nuts 20
mace 27, 29
millet 4, 10, 11
mustard 24, 25, 29

nutmeg 27

oats 4, 10, 11

paprika 28
peanuts 7, 20, 21
pecans 16, 19
pepper 24, 25, 29
pine nuts 17
pistachios 20

rice 4, 14, 15
rye 10

saffron 28, 29
salt 24, 25
sesame 28, 29
sorghum 4, 10, 11
star anise 29

turmeric 28, 29

vanilla 27, 29

walnuts 4, 18, 19
wheat 4, 8, 9, 10, 11
white peppercorns 24
wild rice 15